Help for the Hurting

Surviving the Storms of Life

By

Ryan Sutton

To: Kris

It was great meeting you!
I wish it could have been under
different circumstances. LOL ü
I felt like I'm supposed to
send you a copy of this book
I wrote. I pray it blesses you!
I'm sorry for the loss you &
your family recently experienced.
I'm praying for y'all!
   God Bless You, Ryan

Help For The Hurting

ISBN: 978-1505713299

Copyright © 2015 by Ryan Sutton

ABOUT THE AUTHOR

Ryan Sutton surrendered to the call to preach under the ministry of B.H. Clendennen a few days after his fourteenth birthday in 1997. He preached his first sermon the following Sunday and was ordained to pastor his first church three years later. He has preached in churches and revivals throughout the USA and has ministered internationally in China, Russia, India, Europe, Africa and Latin America. Ryan continues to travel and preach throughout the nation while serving as the senior pastor of The Grace Center, a dynamic multi-cultural church, in Festus, Missouri.

TO ORDER MATERIALS OR SCHEDULE MEETINGS
P.O. Box 21, Crystal City, Missouri 63019
636-465-0885
www.RyanSutton.org |
www.TheGraceCenter.com

This book is dedicated to the strongest people I know:
my mom, Cindy Sutton and my grandma, Snodie
Sutton. Thank you for always believing in me.
I never would have made it without the two of you.
I love you more than words can say.

CONTENTS

Introduction

Power Out of Pain

Life happens. We all have hurts. We all pass through storms. In this booklet, I am going to offer help for those who are having difficulty processing their pain and recovering from their storms. But first, I want to raise two questions that will be addressed later, in greater detail: "Can there be purpose in pain" and "How can we make sense out of the storms of life?"

It's hard to hurt. It's painful to struggle forward through the pain. Sometimes we are tempted to wonder if we will ever recover. But God's grace comes when we feel like we can't go on. We, at first, speak words of faith and claim the victory over sickness, pain or difficult circumstances. But often, like the apostle Paul, we cry out for deliverance. We cry out to God and ask Him to remove the painful thorns of life when the trials drag on. Don't beat yourself up if that is your experience. The devil will try to make you think that you are struggling because you blew it, because of your own mistakes, or because you lack faith. Even if those things were all true, God still isn't going to forsake you. He loves you. He will not reject or condemn you. Refuse the condemnation and lies of the devil and keep believing to see God's goodness, mercy and favor released in your life. His grace will carry you through. When your strength is all used up, it's still not over. His strength will come to pick you up. It doesn't make sense to our natural minds but God's word is true and we accept it by faith, no matter how we feel.

The apostle Paul had more than his share of pain and he passed through countless storms. He prayed in faith when he asked God to remove his "thorn in the flesh" but after a long struggle he realized that it was not going to happen. He also realized that God was not going to leave him alone in the struggle. He sustained him with supernatural strength and sufficient grace. Paul understood that there was a higher purpose in the pain than he was able to fully understand. In such times, all we can do is trust God, move forward by faith and keep looking up. He will not fail us. And if it never makes sense to us on earth, we can still trust our loving Father knowing that, "earth has no sorrow that heaven can't heal."

"And lest I should be exalted above measure by the abundance of the revelations, a thorn in the flesh was given to me, a messenger of Satan to buffet me, lest I be exalted above measure. Concerning this thing I pleaded with the Lord three times that it might depart from me. And He said to me, "My grace is sufficient for you, for My strength is made perfect in weakness." Therefore most gladly I will rather boast in my infirmities, that the power of Christ may rest upon me. Therefore I take pleasure in infirmities, in reproaches, in needs, in persecutions, in

distresses, for Christ's sake. For when I am weak,
then I am strong (2 Corinthians 12:7-10).

We know that the apostle Paul didn't lack faith, yet he passed through many painful periods in his storm-tossed life. Jesus told us we would have tribulation in this world. He also told us to take heart because He had overcome the world (John 16:33). It may not feel like it right now but the truth is, His victory is our victory. Our hurts will be healed, because Jesus has already paid the price. We are destined to overcome. Paul viewed his suffering in the light of eternity. He wants us to understand that blessing and victory are promised to believers not only in this life but in the next.

"For I consider that the sufferings of this present
time are not worthy to be compared with the glory
which shall be revealed in us" (Romans 8:18).

That verse is followed with the promise of companionship and help from the Holy Spirit in every struggle of life. Actually the promise goes beyond the assurance of help. God assures us that even if the pain and struggle is beyond our ability to process or understand, He will somehow cause it all to work for our eternal good.

"Likewise the Spirit also helps in our weaknesses. For we do not know what we should pray for as we ought, but the Spirit Himself makes intercession for us with groanings which cannot be uttered. Now He who searches the hearts knows what the mind of the Spirit is, because He makes intercession for the saints according to the will of God. And we know that all things work together for good to those who love God, to those who are the called according to His purpose" *(Romans 8:26-28).*

Paul continually made declarations of faith in the midst of the trials and troubles of this life. His faith convinced him that God would always be on our side and that nothing could separate us from His love. Believing these things might not make the pain go away, but it does convince us that we are victorious in Christ no matter how we feel.

"What then shall we say to these things? If God is for us, who can be against us? Who shall separate us from the love of Christ? Shall tribulation, or distress, or persecution, or famine, or nakedness, or peril, or sword?... in all these things we are more than conquerors through Him who loved us. For I am persuaded that neither death nor life, nor angels nor principalities nor powers, nor things present nor things to come, nor height nor depth, nor any other created thing, shall be able to separate us from the love of God which is in Christ Jesus our Lord (Romans 8;31, 35-39).

I want to set the tone for what follows by looking at his experiences in Acts 16. Remember the trouble he had in Philippi? He went there full of faith, with clear direction from God but trouble started soon after he got to town. Some will have difficulty accepting the idea that faith and trouble often go together. But no one will question that Paul had great faith, and anyone who has studied his life will agree that "Trouble" may have been his middle name.

There is no doubt that he was in the will of God. While praying for direction, he saw a vision of a man calling, "Come over here and help us." He set out for Philippi knowing that God was leading him.

Shortly after arriving, he cast a demon out of a girl. He was rewarded for that by being beaten and thrown in prison. How could there be any purpose in that pain? Why had a vision from God brought him to prison? None of it made any sense to him but that didn't keep him from praising God at midnight. That praise, offered in the midst of his pain, got God's attention. When the praise went up, the power came down. God caused an earthquake and sent angels to open the doors and unlock the chains. It was definitely an exciting moment but it didn't remove the pain of the beating and arrest.

Power came out of praise offered up during a painful trial of faith. Paul found himself in the middle of a miracle. In the midst of the excitement, it is doubtful that he was trying to perceive the purpose in the pain. But it all started making sense to him when he saw the jailer and heard him say, "Sirs, what must I do to be saved?" The jailer was the man he saw in the vision. He and his entire household, and probably some prisoners, received Jesus and were baptized.

Is the pain of a beating worth the salvation of a soul – several souls? I am sure Paul would think so. He had no problem seeing the purpose in the pain. The heart of the jailer was open to Jesus and God had to get somebody into his world to reach him. Paul was the answer to the jailer's prayers.

There is nothing pleasant about pain. It is not difficult to see the higher purpose in Paul's experience, but not all cases are like that. We often struggle through pain wondering why God doesn't deliver us. We find it difficult to believe that anything positive could come out of it and our natural minds fail to perceive any reason for it. However, we can see positive fruit come from pain:

Pride is broken and humility is born; a greater dependence on God develops; faith grows stronger through testing, and sometimes, as in Paul's case in Philippi, power comes during a struggle with pain and is released through brokenness.

My purpose in this booklet goes beyond trying to understand the "Why" of pain. I offer practical help for those who are hurting. I attempt to do more than make sense out of it; I endeavor to help the hurting recover from it. The same is true of storms. An entire book could be written about why storms come. My purpose here is primarily to help you survive the storms of life and, hopefully, convince you that you can come out better, not bitter. If you are having difficulty bouncing back from the pain of rejection, abuse or betrayal, the following pages will help you. If you are worn out and weary from fighting through storm after storm, you will find new strength and encouragement. God is committed to heal every hurt and bring you through every storm with faith and victory. Let the following words of David from Psalm 27:13-14 encourage you to read on and receive help from the Lord.

"I would have lost heart, unless I had believed that I would see the goodness of the LORD in the land of the living. Wait on the LORD; Be of good courage, And He shall strengthen your heart; Wait, I say, on the LORD."

Chapter One

Help for the Hurting

"Let us therefore come boldly to the throne of grace, that we may obtain mercy and find grace to help in time of need" (Hebrews 4:16).

Are you passing through a season of intense pressure and pain? If not, you probably know others who are. People are hurting everywhere. Our world is filled with pain. For many, it has become almost unbearable. The storms of life just keep coming. Earnest prayer often seems to go unanswered. The pressure keeps building and the temptation to yield to despair can become overwhelming.

Pressure and pain that go on and on can leave us feeling like God has forsaken us but faith tells us that is not true. In these difficult times, we must live by faith, not feelings. We must find strength and encouragement in God's Word.

The children of God are not strangers to pressure and pain. The Bible is filled with victorious accounts of people who survived the storms of life and pressed through the pain by faith. God won't desert us in our time of need. He invites us to come to Him to receive help when we feel overwhelmed. Jesus promised that He would never leave us alone in our problems or our pain. In Hebrews 13:6 we read these comforting words: ***"I will never leave you nor forsake you."*** Just knowing He is with us – even when we don't feel His presence – gives us hope.

Armed with the promises of God, we can face the pressure, problems and pain with hope in our hearts. Are you in a storm? Speak faith in the midst of it – no matter how you feel. Make statements of faith out loud so your brain can hear your own voice proclaiming victory. Say, "With the help of God, I am going over, not under." Declare, "I will not to sink in these troubled waters. Faith is going to carry me to the other side."

If your world is filled with darkness right now, don't give up. The light will shine again. There is hope for everyone who trusts in God. In the midst of the struggle, say out loud, "God is with me. He will strengthen me. With His help, I am going to get through this." You have His word on it.

"Don't be afraid, for I am with you. Don't be discouraged, for I am your God. I will strengthen you and help you. I will hold you up with my victorious right hand" (Isaiah 41:10, NLT).

Maybe you don't feel like you can make it, but you can. You have already come through hell and high water. You didn't think you could get this far, but you did. Something good can still come out of the mess you are in – even if it is a mess of your own making. God is loving and merciful. He is not condemning you for mistakes of the past. He is here to help you. Miracles can come out of messes.

You have survived the pain and by God's grace and mercy you haven't given up. You wouldn't be reading this if you had. You are still holding on to hope. Soon you may come out of the storm and find yourself standing on the shore of possibility with new hope for the future. You will make it if you refuse to quit. Don't despair. The mess may have set you up for a miracle. Good might come out of what looks so bad. *"And we know that all things work together for good to those who love God, to those who are the called according to His purpose" (Romans 8:28).* Don't give up. You may discover that God's power and purpose are waiting to pick you up on the other side of the pain.

Chapter Two

Surviving the Storms of Life

When we think about storms, we have to consider the one the apostle Paul went through on his way to Rome. He was a prisoner sailing on a very troubled sea. Paul's experience can teach us a great deal about making it through the storms of life. He stood up in the midst of the storm by faith and snatched victory out of what looked like certain defeat. The account is so powerful we are going to read most of it before going farther. It is recorded in Acts 27. After we work our way through the storm we will look at a few verses in chapter 28. It will be evident why the devil tried to stop them with the fierce storm. Miracles began soon after they washed up on the shore of an island called

Melita – now Malta. There are miracles ahead but you have to survive the storm to get to them. Don't give up. Storms don't last forever. There is purpose at the end of this thing. You are destined to come out in victory, not defeat.

"Now when much time had been spent, and sailing was now dangerous because the Fast was already over, Paul advised them, [10] saying, "Men, I perceive that this voyage will end with disaster and much loss, not only of the cargo and ship, but also our lives." [11] Nevertheless the centurion was more persuaded by the helmsman and the owner of the ship than by the things spoken by Paul. [12] And because the harbor was not suitable to winter in, the majority advised to set sail from there also, if by any means they could reach Phoenix, a harbor of Crete opening toward the southwest and northwest, and winter there.

[13] When the south wind blew softly, supposing that they had obtained their desire, putting out to sea, they sailed close by Crete. [14] But not long after, a

tempestuous head wind arose, called Euroclydon.*[1]*
[15] So when the ship was caught, and could not head into the wind, we let her drive. *[16]* And running under the shelter of an island called Clauda we secured the skiff with difficulty.
[17] When they had taken it on board, they used cables to undergird the ship; and fearing lest they should run aground on the Syrtis Sands, they struck sail and so were driven. *[18]* And because we were exceedingly tempest-tossed, the next day they lightened the ship. *[19]* On the third day we threw the ship's tackle overboard with our own hands. *[20]* Now when neither sun nor stars appeared for many days, and no small tempest beat on us, all hope that we would be saved was finally given up.

[21] But after long abstinence from food, then Paul stood in the midst of them and said, "Men, you should have listened to me, and not have sailed from Crete and incurred this disaster and loss. *[22]* And now I urge you to take heart, for there will be no loss of life among you, but only of the ship. *[23]* For there stood by me this night an angel of the

God to whom I belong and whom I serve,
²⁴ saying, 'Do not be afraid, Paul; you must be
brought before Caesar; and indeed God has
granted you all those who sail with you.'
²⁵ Therefore take heart, men, for I believe God
that it will be just as it was told me. ²⁶ However, we
must run aground on a certain island."

²⁷ Now when the fourteenth night had come, as we
were driven up and down in the Adriatic Sea,
about midnight the sailors sensed that they were
drawing near some land. ²⁸ And they took
soundings and found it to be twenty fathoms; and
when they had gone a little farther, they took
soundings again and found it to be fifteen
fathoms. ²⁹ Then, fearing lest we should run
aground on the rocks, they dropped four anchors
from the stern, and prayed for day to come. ³⁰ And
as the sailors were seeking to escape from the
ship, when they had let down the skiff into the sea,
under pretense of putting out anchors from the
prow, ³¹ Paul said to the centurion and the
soldiers, "Unless these men stay in the ship, you

cannot be saved." *32 Then the soldiers cut away the ropes of the skiff and let it fall off.*

33 And as day was about to dawn, Paul implored them all to take food, saying, "Today is the fourteenth day you have waited and continued without food, and eaten nothing. 34 Therefore I urge you to take nourishment, for this is for your survival, since not a hair will fall from the head of any of you." 35 And when he had said these things, he took bread and gave thanks to God in the presence of them all; and when he had broken it he began to eat. 36 Then they were all encouraged, and also took food themselves. 37 And in all we were two hundred and seventy-six persons on the ship. 38 So when they had eaten enough, they lightened the ship and threw out the wheat into the sea.

39 When it was day, they did not recognize the land; but they observed a bay with a beach, onto which they planned to run the ship if possible. 40 And they let go the anchors and left them in the *sea, meanwhile loosing the rudder ropes; and they hoisted the mainsail to the wind and made for shore. ⁴¹ But striking a place where two seas met, they ran the ship aground; and the prow stuck fast and remained immovable, but the stern was being broken up by the violence of the waves.*

⁴² And the soldiers' plan was to kill the prisoners, lest any of them should swim away and escape. ⁴³ But the centurion, wanting to save Paul, kept them from their purpose, and commanded that those who could swim should jump overboard first and get to land, ⁴⁴ and the rest, some on boards and some on parts of the ship. And so it was that they all escaped safely to land."

The storm kept getting worse and worse until finally all hope of deliverance was gone. It was a miracle that everyone on board escaped safely to land. They escaped because one man on the ship had faith and took hold of a word from God. This storm had to be even more difficult for

Paul because he was in it as a result of decisions others made. He warned the sailors of impending danger in verse ten and tried to convince them not to set sail. The owner and the captain of the ship ignored his warnings and convinced the Roman centurion who was in charge of Paul and the other prisoners to continue the journey.

Some of us have learned the hard way how dangerous it is to ignore God's warnings. We sailed out on a troubled sea and charted our own course. The beginning of the journey was pleasant, the winds were fair, the sailing was smooth. Others on board the ship with Paul laughed at the crazy preacher with the ominous warnings. But the laughter was short lived. Early in the journey, they realized they were in deep trouble and there was no turning back. The devil had set them up for destruction and they fell right into the trap. That's how he works. He continually tries to get us to take a path that will lead to disaster.

Sometimes storms seem to come out of nowhere. Everything appears to be working out for you but it can all change in a moment. Suddenly the calm winds become fierce and they are beating against your ship with force and fury. You know you are in trouble and you realize it is because you ignored the warnings. Fear takes hold of your heart as the cruel thoughts of pain and loss bombard your mind.

The false peace at the beginning of the journey is gone and seasoned sailors are left trembling, not knowing what to do. Something dark and dreadful hit them with overwhelming force. When they left Crete "the south wind blew softly"(v.13), but soon a "tempestuous wind called Euroclydon" assailed them and started shattering everything around them. The storm produced panic and they would have jumped ship if Paul had not stopped them. The man with faith in his heart rose and took charge. He became the captain of the ship by default. The sailors who at first laughed at him now listened carefully to every word he spoke.

Chapter Three

You Can Still Be Saved After All Hope Is Gone

Did you think you were lost because you lost all hope? You must be listening to the devil. God never told you such a thing. You may have given up on yourself but God hasn't. Things kept getting worse instead of better on the boat and everyone but Paul was ready to give up. But you can't quit in the middle of the ocean. You can't give up while the storm is still raging. You can't quit fighting until the fight is over. When your strength is gone, God's grace will help you. He is not going to give up on you. His strength will come when yours is all used up. You can't go on, but He can. Greater is He Who is in you than he who is in the storm. They were ready to give up in the early part of the storm, but God wasn't ready to give up on them. He got them through the worst of it after all their hope was gone.

"And when neither sun nor stars in many days appeared, and no small tempest lay upon us, all hope that we should be saved was then taken away" (v. 20, KJV).

It was so bad it seems that even Paul momentarily lost hope. He included himself in the sentence. He said "all hope that we should be saved was taken away." But that didn't stop God. He penetrated the darkness and faith rose in Paul's heart. By faith he overcame the despair that threatened to overwhelm him. Paul shows us how to make it through the dark times. He focused on God instead of the darkness and he heard the word of the Lord. That word gave him strength and calmed his troubled soul. He held on to the word by faith and when he spoke it others were encouraged to rise up out of their despair and take action. That's the reason we are reading about this great victory over two-thousand years later. They were never alone. God was with them in the darkness. Their loss of hope didn't prevent Him from helping them. God can redeem our lives from destruction, restore blessing and help us recover.

"Who redeems your life from destruction, Who crowns you with lovingkindness and tender mercies" (Psalm 103:4).

Has a period of darkness left you discouraged? Has it lasted too long? Are you wondering if things are ever going to change? Do you hear voices in the darkness that are often not God's voice? Do you hear thoughts in your head that say, "It's over. All hope is gone?" Those aren't God's thoughts. They are not even your thoughts. They are lies of the devil. He is a master counterfeiter. He makes his thoughts sound like your thoughts. The devil is a liar. God is going to bring you through this thing. It's bigger than you are, and God knows that you need His help. You have done everything you can do but the darkness hasn't lifted and the winds are still blowing. The ship of your life is being shattered and you feel helpless to stop it. What can you do? You can do what Paul did: Trust God, listen for His voice and, when you hear it, speak by faith into the darkness. You are going to get through this by believing, speaking and acting on the word of God.

Sometimes there aren't any explanations for what you are going through. It is difficult to bear the pain; it is more difficult to make any sense out of it. All you can do is lift up your hands, praise him like Paul did, and say, "I trust You. I don't understand but I trust You. It doesn't make any sense but I trust You." There will be victories after the valleys of life but the ultimate victory will be experienced in the next. Faith will help you to remember that even if life on earth is filled with long periods of pain, heaven is on the other side of it.

During the storms of life, we have to exalt the Word of God over everything that is going wrong. That is what Abraham did. After long years of waiting for the fulfillment of the promise, his faith and his patience were sorely tested; but he held on and lived to see the promised blessing. There were painful times before Isaac was born. Abraham's impatience brought Ishmael into the world and resulted in strife between Sarah and Hagar. It got so intense that, at the request of Sarah, Abraham sent Hagar and Ishmael away. That was a sad day for Abraham. His loved Ishmael and it broke his heart to have to make him leave, but he was not the son of promise and there was no other choice. Abraham's attempt to help God fulfill the promise resulted in disaster. There is still strife between the descendants of Isaac and Ishmael to this day.

Abraham's mind was filled with questions and his heart was filled with pain, but he pressed on – and he held on to the promise. Abraham's amazing journey of faith is recorded in Genesis 12 – 25. The record clearly shows that Abraham trusted God through all the painful periods of his life. The promise was greater than the pain. Abraham lived to see the promise fulfilled. He believed God when he didn't know where, how or why. Paul tells us that when he and Sarah were too old to have a child, he kept believing. It was humanly impossible but he knew it could still happen because he believed that all things are possible with God. He didn't deny the natural circumstances; he just believed what God had said more than what the circumstances were saying. When all hope was gone, Abraham held on to the promise by faith.

"Therefore it is of faith that it might be according to grace, so that the promise might be sure to all the seed, not only to those who are of the law, but also to those who are of the faith of Abraham, who is the father of us all (as it is written, "I have made you a father of many nations") in the presence of Him whom he believed—God, who gives life to the dead and calls those things which do not exist as though they did; who, contrary to hope, in hope believed, so that he became the

father of many nations, according to what was spoken, "So shall your descendants be." And not being weak in faith, he did not consider his own body, already dead (since he was about a hundred years old), and the deadness of Sarah's womb. He did not waver at the promise of God through unbelief, but was strengthened in faith, giving glory to God, and being fully convinced that what He had promised He was also able to perform. And therefore "it was accounted to him for righteousness" (Romans 4:17-22).

Chapter Four

You Can Survive Even If Your Ship Sinks

The ship was shattered and sinking but the passengers didn't perish. They had ignored Paul's warnings. They got in this mess all by themselves but God had mercy on them anyway. You don't have to let the devil condemn you. God knows you messed up but He still loves you. He forgives you. He wants to help you. Stop listening to the devil's lies. Stop letting him beat you to death with regrets. Take hold of God's mercy and forgiveness and believe for deliverance one more time. You don't have time to listen to the devil in the midst of your storm. Tell him to shut up in Jesus name and start listening to the Word of God. You are going to live, not die. You may suffer loss but you will not be lost. Your ship may go down but you are not going down with it. You are coming out of this storm and, with the help of God, you will recover. You are not going under; you are going over.

Let's study Paul for awhile instead of the storm. He can teach us how to press through the pain and survive the cruel storms of life. When everyone else was overcome with fear, this amazing man stood up in faith. How could he do that? While others panicked, he prayed and got a word from God. God gave him a promise and he believed it. We read it earlier but it is worth reading again.

"I urge you to take heart, for there will be no loss of life among you, but only of the ship. For there stood by me this night an angel of the God to whom I belong and whom I serve, saying, 'Do not be afraid, Paul; you must be brought before Caesar; and indeed God has granted you all those who sail with you.' Therefore take heart, men, for

*I believe God that it will be just as it was told me"
(v. 22-25).*

By faith – in the midst of the storm – Paul prayed and heard the word of the Lord. When he spoke it in faith, others were strengthened and encouraged. There is power in faith-filled words. We need to speak them in the midst of the storm. That is the time we need to hear them the most. Life and death are in the power of the tongue. Paul believed and, therefore, he spoke. You may not hear a word like Paul did but I assure you God is speaking. You may not see an angel standing beside you but I assure you, he is there. God will not leave you alone in the storms of life.

You don't have to feel his presence or hear His voice to know He is with you. You have His promise and faith says that is enough. We have earlier read the whole account so we know that it played out just as Paul said it would. The whole boatload of unbelievers was saved because there was a man of God on board who believed the Word of the Lord. He couldn't go down with the ship because he had a God-ordained appointment with Caesar in Rome. It was a painful journey but he knew he would get there. Why? Because God said he would and he believed it.

Chapter Five

Desperate Faith

Desperate faith holds on to God with great determination. It lets go of other things but it holds on to God. Desperate faith can turn loose of things it has loved to take hold of something of greater value. "He is no fool who gives up what he cannot keep to gain what he cannot lose" (Jim Elliott, missionary martyr). Paul instructed them to lighten the load as the storm grew worse. They started throwing things overboard. In the midst of a crisis you might have to make the painful decision to let go of things you want to hold on to. You might have to lighten the load.

"Therefore we also, since we are surrounded by so great a cloud of witnesses, let us lay aside every

weight, and the sin which so easily ensnares us, and let us run with endurance the race that is set before us, looking unto Jesus, the author and finisher of our faith, who for the joy that was set before Him endured the cross, despising the shame, and has sat down at the right hand of the throne of God (Hebrews 12:1-2).

Sometimes we have no choice other than to let go of things we want to keep. It can be painful but it is essential to move forward. There is joy before us but, like Jesus, we have to endure some pain on the journey toward it. God wants to help us bear our burdens. He wants to help us in the painful trials of life. He knows how to get us through the pain and carry us toward the fulfillment of His purpose. Sometimes the pressure lets up and it seems that things are getting better. But then, without warning, things start coming apart all around us. That is the very moment God wants us to trust Him the most.

It is not easy to start throwing things overboard. It is difficult to let go. The sense of loss sinks down deep in our hearts. While the storm is raging, when your heart is pierced by the sense of loss, the devil tempts you to give up. But God is always near at such times. He loves you too much to let you face the pain alone. His strength will lift you up and the hope of recovery will again stir in your heart. You may be in a mess you made all by yourself but He still won't let you go. He is not going to give you up to the storm. He is going to carry you through the storm and cast you up on the shore of new possibilities.

Chapter Six

Delivered in the Storm, Not from It

They weren't delivered from the storm; they were delivered in it. They wanted out of it but God had a purpose for letting them pass through it. We feel the same way. We just want God to deliver us. We have difficulty understanding that there may be purpose in our pain. But the process of passing through hard times by faith can bring positive results. It doesn't make sense while we are in the trial but the outcome can be deeper dependence on God which produces stronger faith. We often feel defeated in the storm but God's plan is to bring us out with victory and a greater anointing than we had when we went in. Faith is developed in trials.

" Beloved, do not think it strange concerning the fiery trial which is to try you, as though some strange thing happened to you; but rejoice to the extent that you partake of Christ's sufferings, that when His glory is revealed, you may also be glad with exceeding joy" (1 Peter 4:12-13).

"Who are kept by the power of God through faith for salvation ready to be revealed in the last time. In this you greatly rejoice, though now for a little while, if need be, you have been grieved by various trials, that the genuineness of your faith, being much more precious than gold that perishes, though it is tested by fire, may be found to praise, honor, and glory at the revelation of Jesus Christ" (1 Peter 1:5-6).

Nobody enjoys trials. Nobody wants to pass through periods of pain. To survive the storm, they lightened the load but the ship was broken to pieces anyway. What was the point in throwing things overboard? Lightening the load kept the ship floating until God got Paul where he needed him -

just off the shore of an isolated island filled with lost souls who needed to hear the gospel. The storm seemed like an enemy that would destroy them but God used it to transport Paul exactly where he wanted him.

We don't like to throw things overboard. We don't like to turn loose or let things go. But the pain experienced in the storms of life is sometimes a friend we fail to recognize. If it wasn't for the pain, we would stay committed to things that could hurt us and hold us back for the rest of our lives. God's mercy is in the pain that causes us to disconnect from what has the potential to destroy us. If it wasn't for the storm we might never get rid of the weights that hinder us. We would hold on to things that would eventually sink us.

Determine that you are going to survive the storm no matter what it takes. Tell yourself, "I'm not going down in this storm. I am going to make it to shore. I might have to lose some of my stuff but I am going to make it. I might even lose the ship, but

I am not going to lose my life. I have come through too much to give up now. I didn't think I could make it back then but I did. It doesn't look like I am going to make it now, but I will. My ship might go down but I am not going down with it. I have come too far to go out like this. I am a victor, not a victim. With the help of God, somehow I am going to make it."

When you get into a serious storm, there is often no other choice; you have to let some things go. You have to throw some things overboard. Holding on to something, or someone, that you need to let go of can destroy you. Sometimes your survival depends on letting go of one thing and taking hold of another. No matter how much you love it, no matter how badly you want to hold on to it, you have to let it go if you want to survive the storm. It may be precious to you but you have to let it go. A bag of gold won't help you if you sink holding on to it. A broken board from the shattered ship might be worth more than the gold at the critical moment. You can lose the gold but you must survive. Let go and take hold of the busted board that is going to carry you to shore.

Do you know someone who refused to let go? They knew it wasn't God's will but they were too attached to it. They are still holding on years after they should have disconnected. They are sinking under the weight of it, but they still won't throw it overboard. It has sucked the life out of them. They have become an empty shell with no sense of purpose other than trying to find something to fill the emptiness. God had better plans for them. He had a destiny for their lives. They didn't reach it, all because they couldn't, they wouldn't, let go. They could have survived the storm. They could have recovered from the pain. They could have had a better life but they wouldn't let go. They held on to the thing that the devil sent to sink them. It doesn't have to be that way.

Are you hurting right now because the preceding paragraph is your story? Have you reached the painful valley of regret where you feel that it is too late to recover? Is all hope gone in your world? I have good news for you. It's not too late. If it was, you wouldn't be reading this. You can recover. New hope can rise in your heart. You may be broken, busted and disgusted but God is not – and He still hasn't given up on you. All hope may be gone in your world but it is still alive and well in God's world. Even though you ignored the warnings, even though you held on to what God told you to let go of, there is still hope for you. God is merciful. If you humble yourself and call on His name, He will help you.

You think it is all over. The devil has worked hard to convince you that it is, but the devil is a liar. God has never stopped loving you. In spite of all the sin, in spite of all the painful mistakes, He has not given up on you. He's been there all the time. He knew that the pain would eventually become so great you would return to Him. What have you got to lose? Your ship was shattered in the storm. Your world fell apart around you. Why don't you let go of your world and come into His?

The good news is that you can. He will start the process of healing in your heart the moment you repent and return to Him.

"The Spirit of the LORD is upon Me, Because He has anointed Me To preach the gospel to the poor; He has sent Me to heal the brokenhearted, To proclaim liberty to the captives And recovery of sight to the blind, To set at liberty those who are oppressed; To proclaim the acceptable year of the LORD" (Luke 4:18-19).

"Thus says the Lord of hosts: "Return to Me and I will return to you" (Zechariah 3:18).

Jesus wants to help you. He wants to heal your hurts. He wants to renew your mind and stop the racing thoughts. He wants to help you let go of all the pain of regret and move forward with new hope for life. He wants you to return to Him. He won't reject you. Why? Because He still loves you.

Chapter Seven

There May Be Purpose in Your Pain

Some pain, but not all, may have a positive purpose in your life. The pain that is caused by cruel or negative words seldom has a positive purpose. God can bring good out of bad but we must be careful in this matter. Words are powerful. *"Death and life are in the power of the tongue, and those who love it will eat its fruit' (Proverbs 18:21).* People can bring storms to your life by things they do and with the words they speak. Heaviness can come over you suddenly when someone speaks words over you that minister death. Words can rob you of peace, fill you with fear and cause terrible turmoil in your life. On the other hand, words can minister life. Hope was renewed on a sinking ship, after all hope was gone, because Paul spoke words of faith in the face of darkness and despair. You may know what it is to experience a resurgence of faith in your heart because someone spoke words of life over you. I have witnessed people come out from under a spirit of heaviness because someone spoke life and blessing over them.

The last thing we need in a storm is someone cursing us with negative words spoken to us or over us. This is no small matter. It is a terrible thing to add to someone's heaviness or pain by speaking negative words in a time of crisis. It could sink an already overburdened soul. I pray that God will help us learn to speak words of faith and blessing in the midst of the sorrow and pain, in the midst of the struggle and the storm.

That being said, there is sometimes a purpose in pain, or a purpose for passing through pain. That was the case with Paul in Acts 27 and 28. He suffered pain and loss as a result of being in somebody else's storm. He warned them not to sail but they ignored him. He experienced the same trauma and pain as everyone else on the boat even though he had warned them not to set sail. That didn't stop him from speaking faith into the darkness which caused everyone else on board to find courage to go on. There could have been a different outcome. What do you think would have happened if Paul had let bitterness take hold of him? He would never have been able to hear a word from God. He would have been continually reminding the captain and soldiers that this was not his mess, that he was in it because of their decision: not his. He could have brought the heaviness of death over everyone else by speaking negative words of fear and unbelief. He and everyone on board would have gone down with the ship. It was faith, and positive words spoken in faith, that saved the day.

Paul was actually an innocent victim in the storm. All the pain he experienced came because others had refused to listen to him. It doesn't seem fair that he had to suffer because of the decision others made. But God had a purpose for allowing the pain. We can get overly spiritual when trying to come to grips with the purpose of pain but, the truth is, it can produce positive fruit in our lives. It can test our faith with the result that it becomes stronger; it can produce the fruit of humility and brokenness; it can cause us to develop greater dependence on God: all positives results of pain processed by faith. But there was an even higher purpose in God allowing Paul's pain. Lost souls on an isolated island were going to be saved because God allowed the ship to be blown off course and broken up at sea. They would have sailed on by had the storm not shattered their ship. Malta, in those days, was not high on the list of favorable places to drop anchor.

Sometimes the pain we don't understand has a higher purpose than we are able to comprehend while we are in it. The devil didn't get it. He thought he had succeeded in destroying the apostle he hated with unholy passion. He forgot that he couldn't destroy him because God wasn't finished with him. Paul was ready to go to heaven but he had no intention of laying his body down until God was through with him. He had a word from God about an appointment with Caesar in Rome. Paul was not going to let hell or high water rob him of the opportunity to preach the gospel to Caesar. But God had another assignment for Paul on the way to Rome and allowing the shipwreck was the way He got him there.

Paul himself didn't understand what was going on at first. Sometimes it is hard to make sense out of pain and it seldom helps to talk about a higher purpose in it. Paul had his sights set on Rome and in his mind this was just an unwelcome delay. (He hated unplanned layovers as much as the rest of us). He wasn't thinking about purpose in his pain as he clung desperately to a broken board from the ship, determined to survive the worst storm of his life. That is what you and I must do: survive at all costs. You have to survive until you can succeed. You can't let the pain sink you. You can't go down in this storm. You are tired and hurting. Your ship has been shattered. You have suffered the agony of great loss. Your world has collapsed around you. But you have to go on. God is not finished with you yet. It's bad now but better days are ahead. Victory and blessing may be just around the next bend in the road. The next overwhelming wave may cast you up on the shore of a greater destiny than you ever imagined. It doesn't feel good but there may be purpose in all this pain.

Paul wasn't trying to perceive the purpose in his pain when he stood up on the shore. He was just glad to be alive. I doubt that he was thinking, "I wonder what God has for me on this isolated island?" None of it made any sense. He was just glad that he survived the storm and lived to preach another day. It certainly makes no sense to people who think faith is supposed to keep you out of trouble. Trouble was Paul's middle name and he had discovered, through many painful journeys that God was often right in the middle of it. But purpose in the pain was not on his mind on that distant shore. He was just thinking about how to get off that island and get on with his journey to Rome. I doubt that thoughts of anything significant happening on that little island had even entered his mind. God had other plans.

The great men and women of faith in the Bible, and throughout history, have always been willing to sacrifice passing pleasure on earth for lasting treasure in heaven. In the storms of life, many of them had to disconnect from things they once held dear and move on in life. They had to throw some things overboard. Moses is, perhaps, the best example of them all:

"By faith Moses, when he became of age, refused to be called the son of Pharaoh's daughter, choosing rather to suffer affliction with the people of God than to enjoy the passing pleasures of sin, esteeming the reproach of Christ greater riches than the treasures in Egypt; for he looked to the reward. By faith he forsook Egypt, not fearing the wrath of the king; for he endured as seeing Him who is invisible" (Hebrews 11:24-27).

Moses could have been next in line to be the pharaoh in Egypt, the wealthiest, most powerful country on earth in his day. He could have had all the treasures and pleasures of Egypt. But he rejected position, power, pleasure and prosperity and instead chose "to suffer affliction with the people of God." Why? Why would a man sacrifice so much? He "esteemed the reproach of Christ greater riches than the treasures of Egypt."

With eyes wide open, Moses "by faith forsook Egypt." That decision resulted in him spending forty years as a shepherd in what the Bible calls "the backside of the desert" in the land of Midian. How did he endure those forty years of pain and hard work after living such a luxurious life in the palace? The Bible tells us, in the verses we just read in Hebrews 11:26-27, that he did it by keeping his eyes on the [heavenly] reward and by seeing Him who is invisible.

He saw into the eternal, invisible realm by faith. What he saw made him willing to throw everything this world offered overboard in order to fulfill his purpose, reach his destination, and receive his heavenly reward. Was it worth it? He thought so. The Bible gives ample evidence to show that he made the right decision and that there was a reward waiting at the end of his race on earth. It is clear that Moses didn't perish when his life on earth was done. He passed into the presence of the "Invisible One" he had seen by faith when he forsook Egypt. He appears with Jesus on the Mount of Transfiguration two thousand years after his departure from earth (John17). He is still waiting with Jesus, and the great cloud of witnesses in heaven, to welcome all who finish the race on earth to their heavenly home.

God could have prepared Moses for leadership in the palace of Egypt without sending him to the backside of the desert. But He didn't. We can wonder why it was necessary, but the fact remains: God called the greatest leader of the Old Testament out of the pain and the struggle of the desert, not the comfort and luxury of the palace.

Chapter Eight

Why Did We Have to Lose the Ship?

It can be difficult to recover from great loss. We are tempted to look back and wonder why. In this case, the storm was necessary to get Paul in the vicinity of the lost souls on Malta. The wreck was necessary to get him on Malta. If the ship had survived the storm, they would have sailed on past the island and pressed toward Rome.

What about you? Have you lost a ship or two on the stormy sea of life? Are you looking back with regret or have you made peace under the providence of God? You may be facing loss in a storm right now. What if the storm is not your enemy? Should you be fighting the storm or just fighting to survive it?

Did the past storms you survived permanently hurt you, or did you take something of value out of the painful experience? Your ship was shattered. Your heart was broken. But you survived. The pain of your past didn't destroy you. The storms didn't sink you. Was it all for nothing, or is it possible that what the devil sent to destroy you God has used to develop you?

None of us are exempt from storms, trials, or the pain and pressure of life. Paul had great faith but he passed through periods of hell on earth. We must do the same: Pass through. Someone has said, "If you are walking through hell, keep walking." That's good advice. We must not allow the pressure or the pain to stop us. Are you running out of money before you run out of month? Are bill collectors calling because you missed a payment? That's a storm. Has someone betrayed your trust? Have you gone through the pain of divorce? That's a storm. Is the devil bombarding you with past mistakes? Are you rehearsing regrets and saying things like, "What if? If only? I wish I would have done that. I wish I would not have done that." That is a storm. Do you wake up from a sound sleep with a tormented mind and racing thoughts? Have you suffered financial loss? That is a storm.

You can't go forward looking in the rearview mirror. You can't experience peace in the present if you constantly worry about the future. The devil has a purpose in the storms. He wants to discourage you. He wants you to yield to fear and fall apart. He wants you to lose the strength to press forward because you keep condemning yourself for past mistakes. He wants you to throw your hands up in despair or sit down and quit. He wants to turn up the pressure until you say "I can't take anymore." He wants you to give up. He wants to put thoughts in your mind and deceive you into believing they are your own thoughts. He wants you to believe that you are never going to get through this, that you are never going to make it. But remember: the devil is a liar! You have to make it. God has a purpose for your life. Others are depending on you. You have come too far to give up now.

You can lose your stuff. Throw it overboard if you have to. You can survive without it. But don't lose your hope. That almost sunk the ship Paul was on. Don't go there. Say, I don't care what it takes; I am going to make it to shore. I am not going out like this. I may lose everything but I am going to survive. If I have to swim, float or hang on to this broken board, I am going to make it to shore.

I am leaving my regrets behind. I am pulling pain out by the roots and pushing it away from me. I am saying good-bye to worry. I am going to wash up on this shore free to pursue a new destiny. Yesterday is in the tomb. Tomorrow is in the womb. All I have is now. I don't have to hold on to what God used yesterday to sustain me today. This pain isn't going to kill me. This loss isn't going to do me in. The devil got my stuff but he didn't get my faith. I will rise again and rebuild.

Nothing, no one, is going to stop me. The people on assignment from the devil are not going to mess with me. They may speak death over me but I will push it back with the force of resurrection life. I won't listen to their negative words. I won't come under it. I survived and I am going to keep on surviving until I succeed. I am going to speak life and blessing over me, over my family. I am not going to let people who speak death mess with me.

I lost my ship but I'm not going to trip over it. None of these things are going to move me. I am going to make it. I am going to speak words of faith. I am going to speak to the darkness and to the storm. I am a victor, not a victim.

"What then shall we say to these things? If God is for us, who can be against us" (Romans 8:31)? "In all these things we are more than conquerors through Him who loved us" (Romans 8:37).

"Who shall separate us from the love of Christ? Shall tribulation, or distress, or persecution, or famine, or nakedness, or peril, or sword"

(Romans 8:35)? For I am persuaded that neither death nor life, nor angels nor principalities nor powers, nor things present nor things to come, nor height nor depth, nor any other created thing, shall be able to separate us from the love of God which is in Christ Jesus our Lord" (Romans 8:38-39).

Chapter Nine

Shake It Off

*"Now when they had escaped, they then found out
that the island was called Malta. [2] And the natives
showed us unusual kindness; for they kindled a
fire and made us all welcome, because of the rain
that was falling and because of the cold. [3] But
when Paul had gathered a bundle of sticks and
laid them on the fire, a viper came out because of
the heat, and fastened on his hand. [4] So when the
natives saw the creature hanging from his hand,
they said to one another, "No doubt this man is a
murderer, whom, though he has escaped the sea,
yet justice does not allow to live." [5] But he shook
off the creature into the fire and suffered no
harm. [6] However, they were expecting that he*

would swell up or suddenly fall down dead. But after they had looked for a long time and saw no harm come to him, they changed their minds and said that he was a god.

[7] In that region there was an estate of the leading citizen of the island, whose name was Publius, who received us and entertained us courteously for three days. [8] And it happened that the father of Publius lay sick of a fever and dysentery. Paul went in to him and prayed, and he laid his hands on him and healed him. [9] So when this was done, the rest of those on the island who had diseases also came and were healed. [10] They also honored us in many ways; and when we departed, they provided such things as were necessary" (Acts 28:1-10).

What are the odds of surviving a shipwreck only to be bitten soon after by a deadly viper? The devil must have really hated the apostle Paul. He was obsessed with destroying him but every attempt backfired. Paul refused to die until God was finished with him. The bite of a deadly viper must have been painful. How could there be any purpose in that kind of pain? It sure got the attention of the natives. Paul simply shook the venomous beast off into the fire and went about his business. When some time had passed and Paul had not fallen down dead, the natives changed their opinion of him. He was raised from the sinner category to god status. The whole island was open to him.

We will note the miracles that followed in a moment. First I want to ask you if anything is holding on to you that needs to be shaken off? Has anything attached itself to you that needs to be dropped in the fire? Get rid of it. Let it go. Shake it off. Are you in a relationship that is not the will of god? Let it go. Are you holding on to something that is hurting your walk with the Lord? Lay it down. Did something evil attach itself to you while you were somewhere you shouldn't have been? Shake it off. You have to survive. God is not finished with you yet. Letting go may be painful but it is needful. You can move from pain to power through grace and faith. God hasn't given up on you. Your best days are before you if you will disconnect from the thing that is holding you back and move forward in faith to do the will of God.

Paul moved out of pain into power. The leading resident of the island, a man named Publius, heard about the "god" who shook off poisonous snakes into the fire and lived to testify about it. His father was sick and he decided to ask Paul to make a house call. His father was healed and the result was that every sick person on the island came to have Paul lay his hands on them. My friend Jeff Clark says, "The hand that was bitten is the same hand that later released healing to the multitudes." A revival that swept across the entire island resulted from a shipwreck and a snake bite. Maybe there is purpose in pain that is processed by faith! The demons which had ruled that island were thrown into turmoil. I wonder if the entire population was converted after seeing the miracles and hearing Paul's preaching?

Paul survived the storm and prevailed through the pain. We need to remember what was on the other side of the storm. When we are passing through one of life's cruel storms, we need to do more than survive. We need to come out fighting mad and burning with zeal to pursue God's purpose. There may be miracles in your future. You haven't lasted this long for nothing. You haven't survived all these storms for no reason. There is purpose in your pain. Determine that you are going to do what Paul did: Move from pain to power. Believe that the fierce storms the devil sent to destroy you have instead cast you up on the shore of God's purpose. Paul pressed through the pain and came out of the storm with miracle working power. Think about it: Multitudes were saved and healed because Paul refused to sit down and feel sorry for himself. He refused to let the sorrow of loss weigh him down. He stood up, took a deep breath and got busy doing the will of God. He didn't waste time nursing his pain or trying to figure it all out.

He forgot what was behind and moved forward by faith. He saw opportunity and seized it. The result was lost souls saved. Multitudes who had never heard the gospel became believers. Was the outcome worth the pain? It was to an apostle whose heart beat with love for the lost. How many people in succeeding generations were saved because a storm spit a tough apostle out on their island many years before? How many are in heaven today because Paul fought his way to their shore and stood up to preach at the first opportunity.

You can't let the pain push you down into despair. You can't lie down and let the storm swallow you. You may be hurting now but what is waiting for you just past this storm? You have to live to prove that there can be purpose in pain. You have to survive to show a world full of hurting people that the worst storm of your life can spit you out right into the center of God's will. It may be hard. The funds may be low and the debts may be high. You may want to smile but find it easier to sigh. You may be limping along with a broken heart trying to make sense of all the pain. But you can't stop now. If you are walking through hell there is only one intelligent thing to do: Keep walking. You have to live until you believe Romans 8:28, and then you have to keep living to convince others that it is true. You have to help others believe that it is true: Something good can come out of something bad.

"And we know that all things work together for good to those who love God, to those who are the called according to His purpose."

Who put Paul on that island: God or the devil? If it was the devil, he sure messed up. Was it the storm? Was Paul just a helpless victim of cruel circumstance or was God in the storm? The storm was a bad deal by itself, but God can take a negative and turn it into a positive. All he needs is somebody who will stand up in the middle of the mess and speak His word with authority and faith. Paul was in the whole mess because of mistakes that others had made. It didn't matter. God put him right where he wanted him. The mistakes didn't negate the force of faith. A tired traveler who had survived shipwreck and snakebite stood up in faith and released the fires of revival in the devil's neighborhood. Paul was worn out, cold, and shivering in a body wracked with pain. But none of it moved him. He spit on the trials and rose up in supernatural power to rain on the devil's parade.

I want to be motivated by this powerful apostle. I want to be gripped with the sense of heavenly purpose that kept him pressing toward the goal. I am amazed at the way he continually turned what looked like certain defeat into incredible victory. We previously wondered how many people on that island were saved in succeeding generations. I think it's even bigger than that. I wonder how many missionaries went out from that island through the years to carry the gospel to other parts of the world. Only heaven knows the impact of the greatest soul winner in history on an out of the way island, all because he refused to surrender to a storm. What seemed like a tragic loss of ship and cargo resulted in eternal gain. The incredible events that took place on Malta left the devil shaking his head in dismay. He stirred up a storm to destroy the servant of God but faith transformed it into a current that carried him forward into God's purpose. The storm was costly. There was great loss but it resulted in greater gain: the salvation of lost souls on a distant island.

"He is no fool who gives up what he cannot keep to gain what he cannot lose" (Jim Elliott)

Chapter Ten

His Promise Is Greater Than Your Pain

You may be in the worst storm of your life. You may be experiencing the deepest pain you have ever known. You may be passing through darkness so great all hope is gone. I have good news for you. You can make it. You don't have to sink in the storm. You don't have to perish in your pain. You don't have to die in the darkness. You are not alone. God is with you to deliver you. He can bring you through it all. You, like Peter, may be going down for the last time. But if you call out to Jesus, he will save you. He will lift you up and walk back to the boat with you.

There is hope for you, even if you are in a storm of your own making. I have been in a few. I have experienced shipwrecks and train wrecks. I felt like it was all over. In my mind it was; but God had a different mind. It looked like destruction to me but Jesus came at the moment of my greatest need and said, "It's not over for you. I am not finished with you yet." He never condemned me. He is full of grace and mercy. Don't listen to the devil's lies. In your darkest moments, hold on to the promises of God's word. His promise is greater than your pain. His grace is greater than your sin. His mercy is greater than your mistakes.

"Who forgives all your iniquities, Who heals all your diseases, Who redeems your life from destruction, Who crowns you with lovingkindness and tender mercies" (Psalm 103).

Your little boat may be getting beat to death on the stormy sea of life, but you are going to make it. Jesus is in your boat. It's not going under as long as He is in it. If he gets out, get out with Him. The devil will hammer you with thoughts that you are in a storm because of your own mistakes, because you got out of God's will. The devil is a liar. But even if you are in it because of your own mistake, you still don't have to sink. Jesus will help you if you let Him. The truth is, you might be in a storm and still be in the center of God's will. You might be right where God wants you. The devil set you up for destruction but God over ruled him and set you up for a miracle. This storm might spit you out on a distant shore filled with destiny where power and purpose await you.

There is a reason you must survive the storm. There is a reason you must press through the pain. Others are depending on you. Others need you more than you know. That is why the devil works so hard to convince you that you are insignificant, that what you say and do won't make much difference. The devil is a liar. Somebody is in deeper water than you and God is going to use you to help him. Somebody standing a little farther down the road you are travelling doesn't know Jesus. She is in deeper waters than you. She needs you to press through your pain and get to her before it's too late. She needs to meet somebody who made it through so she can believe that she can make it too. God has a purpose for your life. I don't care how far down you are right now. God hasn't given up on you. He wants to help you get up and move forward with hope in your heart.

Purpose is found on the other side of pain and you always encounter God's power when you arrive at His purpose. It doesn't matter how you got here. It may have been a long, hard journey. You may have come through fire and rain, hell and high water. It doesn't matter: You are here now and God has something for you to do. You survived. You made it. The devil didn't want you to get this far but you did. The storm he sent to destroy you only made you stronger. You just don't know it yet. The pain he sent to crush you didn't do its job. It just made you more compassionate and tender toward others. You feel weak and broken. That's alright. God's strength can be made perfect in your weakness. He uses broken things. Broken vessels who are not impressed with themselves are what He likes to flow through.

There is help for the hurting. God is helping you so you can help others. Your pain has not been without purpose. You are moving from pain to power. Your storms have not been without significance. You survived them and now you can give hope to other storm tossed travelers. Leave your fear behind and go forward in faith to fulfill your destiny. God will help you.

"Do not be afraid, for I have ransomed you. I have called you by name; you are mine. When you go through deep waters, I will be with you. When you go through rivers of difficulty, you will not drown. When you walk through the fire of oppression, you will not be burned up; the flames will not consume you. For I am the LORD, your God, the Holy One of Israel, your Savior" (Isaiah 43:1-3, NLT).

Chapter Eleven

Forward Ever, Backward Never

I made the statement earlier, "If you are walking through hell, keep walking." Now I want to encourage you to add this to that statement: "Keep looking up." You are a pilgrim on this earth. You are just passing through. Some of the pain of this life will never make sense until we reach our eternal home. Remember, "Earth knows no sorrow that heaven can't heal." Even Abraham, the father of faith, experienced pain and heartache in this world. He processed a lot of it by keeping his eyes on the goal. Hebrews 11:10 tells us, ***"For he looked for a city which hath foundations, whose builder and maker is God.***

Paul did the same thing. He suffered some losses in this life. He had to overcome a lot of pain and regret. His mind was bombarded with the pain of past mistakes. He thought he was doing the right thing by severely persecuting Christians. He was responsible for many being beaten, cast into prison and even killed. He presided over the stoning of Stephen. He was obsessed with destroying Christianity until he met Jesus on the road to Damascus. His former hatred for Christians is captured in his discourse before King Agrippa in Acts 26:9-11:

"Indeed, I myself thought I must do many things contrary to the name of Jesus of Nazareth. This I also did in Jerusalem, and many of the saints I shut up in prison, having received authority from the chief priests; and when they were put to death, I cast my vote against them. And I punished them often in every synagogue and compelled them to blaspheme; and being exceedingly enraged against them, I persecuted them even to foreign cities."

We can only imagine the remorse Paul must have felt once he realized his tragic mistakes. He would have sunk down under the weight of despair if not for the mercy of Jesus. By God's grace, he was able to receive forgiveness and to forgive himself. But he still experienced a lot of pain afterwards. His former friends and associates not only rejected him; they did everything in their power to destroy him. He had to walk away from everything he had worked so hard to attain. He lost his power and influence in the Jewish community and became an outcast. Many times he had to flee for his life. Through it all he remained true to the high and holy calling on his life and he remained faithful to the heavenly vision. He tells us how he did it in Philippians 3:7-8 and 12-14:

"But what things were gain to me, these I have counted loss for Christ. Yet indeed I also count all things loss for the excellence of the knowledge of Christ Jesus my Lord, for whom I have suffered the loss of all things, and count them as rubbish,

that I may gain Christ… I press on, that I may lay hold of that for which Christ Jesus has also laid hold of me. Brethren, I do not count myself to have apprehended; but one thing I do, forgetting those things which are behind and reaching forward to those things which are ahead, I press toward the goal for the prize of the upward call of God in Christ Jesus."

He did it by purposing to forget the pain of the past and by pressing forward to the possibilities of the future: "but one thing I do, forgetting those things which are behind and reaching forward to those things which are ahead." Paul kept his eyes fixed on the heavenly prize. He was convinced that it was worth more than all the sacrifice, pain and struggle required to reach it.

He describes the pain and struggle of pressing onward and upward toward the heavenly prize in 2 Corinthians 4:7-9:

"But we have this treasure in earthen vessels, that the excellence of the power may be of God and not of us. We are hard-pressed on every side, yet not crushed; we are perplexed, but not in despair; persecuted, but not forsaken; struck down, but not destroyed— [We know] that He who raised up the Lord Jesus will also raise us up with Jesus, and will present us with you."

Paul drew strength from the spiritual realm to keep pressing forward in faith. He overcame the obstacles and found help for the hard times in prayer and the Word. He lived with eternal perspective. He processed the pain of life in this world by seeing past it to the "joy that was set before him." He ran the race with heaven in his heart and on his mind. His attitude was that no amount of sacrifice or suffering in this temporary life on earth could compare to the eternal reward waiting for believers in heaven.

"Therefore we do not lose heart. Even though our outward man is perishing, yet the inward man is being renewed day by day. For our light affliction, which is but for a moment, is working for us a far more exceeding and eternal weight of glory, while we do not look at the things which are seen, but at the things which are not seen. For the things which are seen are temporary, but the things which are not seen are eternal" (2 Corinthians 4:16-18).

Paul's advice to the weary runner in the race of life is: Keep running and keep looking up as you run. When you get to heaven you will see that it has been worth it all. In Philippians 3:14 we read these words; "I press toward the goal for the prize of the upward call of God in Christ Jesus." This verse implies that the goal is noble and demands our best effort; the calling is to something higher which inspires us to look up when we become weary on the journey; the reward is heavenly and of far greater value than anything on the earth. In other words, it is worth more than all the effort, sacrifice, pain and struggle required to reach it. Here are Paul's words to his spiritual son Timothy, written from a Roman prison as he awaited martyrdom. It is evident that his impending death was not foremost in his thoughts; faith had him thinking about the heavenly reward just past death's door. He didn't even use the word "death." He simply told Timothy that the time of his departure had come. Death was just a passageway from earth to heaven. We should draw strength and courage from his words. He didn't fear death; he welcomed it.

"For I am already being poured out as a drink offering, and the time of my departure is at hand. I have fought the good fight, I have finished the race, I have kept the faith. Finally, there is laid up for me the crown of righteousness, which the Lord, the righteous Judge, will give to me on that Day, and not to me only but also to all who have loved His appearing" (2 Timothy 4:6-8).

With such an attitude, it is not difficult to understand why Paul was willing to exert great effort to continually press toward the prize. The word "press" used in Philippians 3:14 implies great effort and exertion of strength to break through resistance. This heavenly prize of such great value can be received in no other way. There is resistance along the road that leads upward to heaven. There are enemies who try to discourage us and hinder our forward progress. They fight us every step of the way in an attempt to stop us and take us out of the race. But we can overcome all of them with faith that helps us look up and fix our eyes on Jesus. By faith we run and by faith we overcome.

"You are of God, little children, and have overcome them, because He who is in you is greater than he who is in the world" (1 John 4:4). "For whatever is born of God overcomes the world. And this is the victory that has overcome the world—our faith." (1 John 5:4).

We run with the assurance that a heavenly prize is waiting for us when we finish our race on the earth. We saw that the apostle Paul called the prize a crown of righteousness in 2 Timothy 4:8. The apostle James described it as the crown of life: *"Blessed is the man who endures temptation; for when he has been approved, he will receive the crown of life which the Lord has promised to those who love Him" (James 1:12).* The apostle Peter called it a crown of glory: *"and when the Chief Shepherd appears, you will receive the crown of glory that does not fade away (1 Peter 5:4).*

Peter uses rich language to describe our heavenly reward in his first epistle. With that description as a backdrop, he tells us why we can rejoice even as we pass through difficulty and pain on earth.

"Blessed be the God and Father of our Lord Jesus Christ, who according to His abundant mercy has begotten us again to a living hope through the

resurrection of Jesus Christ from the dead, to an inheritance incorruptible and undefiled and that does not fade away, reserved in heaven for you, who are kept by the power of God through faith for salvation ready to be revealed in the last time. In this you greatly rejoice, though now for a little while, if need be, you have been grieved by various trials, that the genuineness of your faith, being much more precious than gold that perishes, though it is tested by fire, may be found to praise, honor, and glory at the revelation of Jesus Christ" (1 Peter 1: 3-7).

"Our ultimate victory is waiting for us on the other side. In heaven, we will say with Moses, Paul, and the great cloud of witnesses already there, "It was worth it all."

"Now I saw a new heaven and a new earth, for the first heaven and the first earth had passed away. Also there was no more sea. Then I, John, saw the holy city, New Jerusalem, coming down out of heaven from God, prepared as a bride adorned for

her husband. And I heard a loud voice from heaven saying, "Behold, the tabernacle of God is with men, and He will dwell with them, and they shall be His people. God Himself will be with them and be their God. And God will wipe away every tear from their eyes; there shall be no more death, nor sorrow, nor crying. There shall be no more pain, for the former things have passed away" (Revelation 21: 1-4).

"And He showed me a pure river of water of life, clear as crystal, proceeding from the throne of God and of the Lamb. In the middle of its street, and on either side of the river, was the tree of life, which bore twelve fruits, each tree yielding its fruit every month. The leaves of the tree were for the healing of the nations. And there shall be no more curse, but the throne of God and of the Lamb shall be in it, and His servants shall serve Him. They shall see His face, and His name shall be on their foreheads. [5] There shall be no night there: They need no lamp nor light of the sun, for

the Lord God gives them light. And they shall reign forever and ever" (Revelation 22:1-4).

"Earth knows no sorrow that heaven can't heal"

*****

Made in the
USA
Middletown, DE